5/06

D0536901

DOGS

GERMAN SHEPHERDS

STUART A. KALLEN

ABDO & Daughters

Published by Abdo & Daughters, 4940 Viking Drive, Suite 662,
Edina, Minnesota 55435.

Library bound edition distributed by Rockbottom Books,
Pentagon Tower, P.O. Box 36036, Minneapolis, Minnesota
55435.

Published 1995
Printed in the United States of America
Second Printing 2002

Cover Photo credit: Peter Arnold, Inc.

Interior Photo credits: Peter Arnold, Inc.

Edited by Rosemary Wallner

Library of Congress Cataloging-in-Publication data

Kallen, Stuart A., 1955   German shepherd / Stuart A. Kallen.
     p. cm. — (Dogs)
     Includes bibilographical references (p.24) and index.
     ISBN 1-56239-454-1 5-24-06
1. German shepherd dogs—Juvenlle literature. [1. German shepherd dogs. 2.
Dogs.] I. Tltle. II. Serles Kallen, Stuart A., 1955- Dogs.
SF429.G37K35 1995
636.7'37—dc20   95-4038
                                                            CIP
                                                            AC

ABOUT THE AUTHOR
Stuart Kallen has written over 80 children's books,
including many environmental science books.

CONTENTS

DOGS AND WOLVES: CLOSE COUSINS

Dogs have been living with humans for more than 12,000 years. Today, hundreds of millions of dogs live in the world. Over 400 **breeds** exist.

All dogs are related to the wolf. Some dogs—like tiny poodles or Great Danes—may look nothing like the wolf. But under their skin, every dog shares many feelings and **traits** with the wolf.

All dogs are related to the wolf.

GERMAN SHEPHERDS

In the 1890s, a German named Captain Max von Stephanitz started a club to **breed** a special German **herding** dog. He picked the smartest and strongest dogs and bred them. Soon a new dog breed—the German shepherd—came into being.

The German shepherd was soon brought to America. At first they were used as sheep dogs. But they proved to be good at many tasks. Some German shepherds were used as police and army dogs.

During World War II, German shepherds were used in the army. The dogs sniffed out bombs and enemies. They also carried medicine and supplies. Today, German shepherds rank among the most popular dogs in America. They are strong, smart, **loyal** dogs that have earned many honors.

German shepherds are strong, smart dogs that make great pets.

WHAT THEY'RE LIKE

German shepherds make lovable pets. They are strong and graceful. They can also be hard workers.

German shepherds have a keen sense of smell. They get to know things by sniffing everything around them. They can easily sniff out objects and people.

Police officers have trained German shepherds to catch criminals. Other people have trained these dogs for search-and-rescue work. German shepherds can climb ladders, ride in helicopters, and move across rough ground.

People have also trained German shepherds as **Seeing Eye dogs**. They help people who are blind.

Police train German shepherds to catch criminals.

COAT AND COLOR

German shepherds have double **coats** to keep them warm. The medium hair of the thick outer coat is straight. The wiry undercoat keeps water and cold from reaching the skin. Shepherds are usually brown and black.

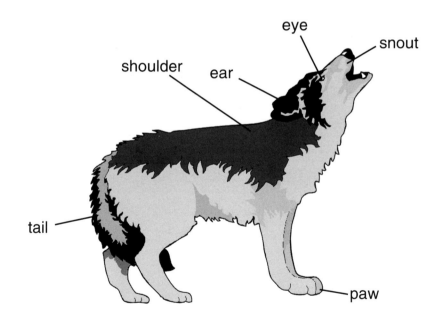

All dogs share the same features with their common ancestor, the wolf.

German shepherds have double coats that keep them warm in the winter.

SIZE

The adult German shepherd is about 25 inches (63 cm) from the ground to its shoulders. Males weigh 75 to 85 pounds (34 to 39 kg). Females weigh 60 to 70 pounds (27 to 31kg).

The German shepherd's **muzzle** is shaped like a long wedge. The shepherd's large ears are turned forward and erect. Its almond-shaped eyes are alert and dark. The German shepherd moves with a graceful, flowing walk. When the dog runs, few animals can catch it.

The German shepherd's muzzle is shaped like a long wedge.

CARE

German shepherds are amazing dogs, but they are not for everybody. They are too big for tiny apartments. They can be hard to handle unless properly trained. And they eat a lot of food.

Like all dogs, shepherds need the same things that humans need: a warm bed, food, water, exercise, and lots of love.

German shepherds have long hair that needs to be brushed every day. If the dog is not brushed, its beautiful **coat** will become matted and tangled. Sometimes, the dog will need a bath and its nails clipped. All dogs need shots every year. These shots stop diseases such as **distemper** and **hepatitis**.

As a member of your household, your dog expects love and attention. Shepherds enjoy human contact and like to **retrieve** sticks or catch Frisbees.

German shepherds have long hair that needs to be brushed every day.

FEEDING

Like all dogs, German shepherds like meat. But shepherds need a well-balanced diet. Most dog foods—dry or canned—will provide the dog with the proper **nutrition**.

When you buy a puppy, find out what it has been eating and continue that diet. A small puppy needs four to five small meals a day. By six months, it will need only two meals a day. By one year, a single evening feeding will be enough.

Shepherds must be exercised every day so they do not gain weight. Walking, running, and playing will keep your dog happy and healthy. Give your dog a hard rubber ball with which to play.

Like any animal, a shepherd needs fresh water. Keep water next to the dog's food bowl and change it daily.

German shepherds need a well-balanced diet.

THINGS THEY NEED

Dogs need a quiet place to sleep. A soft dog bed in a quiet corner is the best place for a German shepherd to sleep. German shepherds can live indoors or outdoors. If the dog lives outside, give it a dry, **insulated** dog house.

Shepherds love to run. A fenced-in yard is the perfect home for the dog. If that is not possible, use a chain on a runner.

In most cities and towns, dogs need to be leashed when going for a walk. Dogs also need a license. A dog license has the owner's name, address, and telephone number on it. If the dog runs away, the owners can be called.

In most cities and towns, dogs need to be leashed when going for a walk.

PUPPIES

Average German shepherds can have three to five puppies at one time. The dog is **pregnant** for about nine weeks. When she is ready to give birth, she needs a dark place away from noises. If your dog is pregnant, give her a strong box lined with an old blanket. She will have her puppies there.

Puppies are tiny and helpless when born. They arrive about half an hour apart. The mother licks them clean and helps them start breathing. Their eyes are shut, making them blind for their first nine days. They are also deaf for about ten days.

Dogs are **mammals**. This means they drink milk from their mother. After four weeks, puppies will grow teeth. Separate them from their mother and give the puppies soft dog food.

German shepherd puppies have sturdy bodies with thick, soft fur.

GLOSSARY

BREED - A group of animals with the same traits.

COAT - A dog's outer covering (fur).

DISTEMPER (dis-TEMP-pur) - A disease of dogs and certain other animals, caused by a virus.

HEPATITIS (hep-uh-TIE-tis) - The swelling of the liver caused by a virus.

HERD - To form into a group.

INSULATION (in-sue-LAY-shun) - Something that stops heat loss.

LOYAL - True and faithful to someone.

MAMMAL - A group of animals, including humans, that have hair and feed their young milk.

MUZZLE - The jaws, mouth, and nose of an animal.

NUTRITION (new-TRISH-un) - Food; nourishment.

PEDIGREE - A chart that lists a dog's ancestors.

PREGNANT - With one or more babies growing inside.

RETRIEVE - To return or bring back.

SEEING EYE DOG - Dogs trained to lead the blind.

TRAIT - A feature or characteristic.

Index

BIBLIOGRAPHY

American Kennel Club. *The Complete Dog Book*. New York: Macmillan, 1992.

Clutton-Brock, Juliet. *Dog*. New York: Alfred A. Knopf, 1991.

The Complete Book of the Dog. New York: Holt, Rinehart, & Winston, 1985.

Green, Carl R., and William R. Sanford. *The German Shepherd*. New York: Crestwood House, 1990.

Sylvester, Patricia. *The Reader's Digest Illustrated Book of Dogs*. New York: The Reader's Digest Association, 1984.